Love Has Fallen

Love Has Fallen

Luscious Words for Modern-day Romantics

by
Gustavo Lapis Ahumada

Eloquent Books
New York, New York

Eloquent Books
An imprint of AEG Publishing Group
845 Third Avenue, 6th Floor—6016
New York, NY 10022
http://www.eloquentbooks.com

ISBN: 978-1-60860-233-9

Book Designer: Bruce Salender

Printed in the United States of America.

To my Daughter Trinity

"… May Love show you its kinder side."

I want to thank all the souls I have come to know and love in this brief, brittle sea of mishap. I have lived and I have loved. This I can say with a clear, clean heart.

I am grateful for the glory of love that I have been fortunate enough to call my own. Just as I am equally grateful for the achingly beautiful suffering at the hands of love lost.

…For if it were not for the thorns, honey would hardly be worth licking.

CONTENTS

A Melody?

You want someone to offer you a melody
I can't help but to wonder why?
If my words could set your thoughts on fire,
Would you let them?
Or would you let the past hush my words?
If you are who I think you are
Then the moment has come for me to be set free
Of this cold place
I may not be beautiful, but this Melody will be
It is the song of things to come and love eternal
A tempo slow enough for two
A melody that only you and I can hear
Sit back and close your eyes,
Listen to the quiet
Listen to this song
This song I cry for you
I'm not sure if the melody will move you
But it's what I do
It is who I am
It is what you bring out in me
It is in the gleam of my scars
Me, I'm always at the bottom of some ocean
You, you have the stars in your eyes
If you are who I think you are
Then the moment has come for me to surface
To disrobe solitude and lift healing hands,
Golden and wanting
Sit back and close your eyes
Listen to the fading echo
With fragile breath and somber hum

Gustavo Lapis Ahumada

I offer myself to you
At the rear of your thoughts
Behind your forgotten veils
I will hum this solemn tune just for you
I reach for your hand and hope
that you will understand me
You want someone to offer you a melody?
Well, here is one from a wretched heart
Sit back and close your eyes
This Melody is just for you

Distraction

I gaze upon you, enthralled
Like stars in Moonlight's beam
You turn away, uninterested and barren
My quiet heart is neither graceful nor elegant
But the sense of my distraction most certainly is
I want to hold you -- close
Perhaps share hopes and fears a like
Embracing you -- a new sense security
Trembling with temptation -- a kiss
My lips to your lips
My lips to your eyes
Cascading down your back
My kiss -- relentless and showering
But you are always a breath away
You are always a dream away

The Greater Adoration

You enter like soft dusk on gray day
Your smile -- a storming legion of angels
The cold fortress I once called heart - falls
You cast a fragile shadow across something
already long gone
The cold sneaks into me with a pride suitable of
someone like you
I see you there, somewhere in the deep
Something is going to happen - I fear
Worst yet, I fear that nothing will
I see you before me
Something of a dream I held long ago
Long ago in a time when I had the courage
to dream of great things
Of beautiful things
Of you
A thousand heavens for your kiss
Sacred must be the soul that moves me as
only you do
I see you and I speak to you but you are deaf
to my tender words
I understand that your interests lay with
someone else
But it does not calm the pain nor does it quiet
The blinding maelstrom
What I would do for a chance to hold you
To wake in your arms
To feel your hands on my face,
To welcome a kiss from your lips
You have become as vast as the pale horizon

in my cold shallow sky and just as unreachable
My skies are not enough for you, why?
I will silence my sorrow
I will do my best to hold onto what is left of my
Dignity, my pride
For it is all that I have
I surrender myself to a blind God and
The greater adoration
You, my beautiful slow dive, just you
It is a sad thing when a singular coincidence –
You and I
Becomes a blazing thing of fire and hope,
Only to end in a tragic descent of
pale disappointment
To kiss you,
    ... Oh my god, just to kiss you

Pure Heart

We trade quiet famished stares
We operate in the art of desolate sighs
Our tears compliment one another
You are shadow and undercurrent
On a head-on collision with a Firestorm
Your fall from grace was no accident
It is no deterrent
I take you as you are with no promise
I'm not sure of the outcome
I do not need to be sure
For your kiss I will gladly cast caution
to the wind
It is by your side that destiny calls
It is by your side that I choose this path
I raise my hand to the sky
Hold breath and sing your name
With a clear head and pure heart
I summon thee

Gustavo Lapis Ahumada

The Quiet in the Water Stirs

Courage! And hold the line
I tell myself as I come face to face
with Love's scathing dominion
I reach out to you sensing your fear
Fear not my love
Tonight is not a night for the weak hearted
Blood upon blood
This time love comes for our souls
I quietly summon faith
Be with me, stay by my side
For love may have forsaken us
But it has failed to break our spirit
Rise with me
Stars will be measured by what we do here today
Do not fear the doom at hand
Let yourself be stripped of all possessions
So that no one may lay claim to your soul
Let the word of faith dance sprightly
upon your tongue
Let passion's ardent splendor
burn deep in your heart
Love fiercely, Love madly
Embrace the worse to come
For love is loss in its ultimate design
At the turn of the tide there will be no escape
But there will be no need to escape
Take my hand
Embrace this flood with no reservations
Bleed with me
Love fiercely, Love madly
Embrace the Love to come

Casting Flowers

If there exist a place, somewhere far away
A place where I can close my eyes and tell you
how much I appreciate you
The beauty and the indigo essence of your being
Without being inappropriate
Without disrespecting the one close to your
Heart, the one close to my heart
A place where I can sigh without fear
and smile somewhat in your direction
A place where I can just observe and absorb you
From your piercing eyes
Down to your perfect toes
If such a place should exist
I would be the one standing by the water's edge
Casting flowers for things that will never be

My Sweet

Hold your crimson tongue
Mind your words foul
I know you thirst but this is not your time
Free your slave, let him breathe
There is much work to be done
Ride your stallion across moonlit bays
Your throat holds empty promises
There is no Fire for you here tonight

Days of Never

Never thought it would be like this
So cold and so numbing
Life without you has lost its shimmer
Songs without you have lost all grace
Days drudge by like winter's molasses
Stolen thoughts of you do little to warm my
lost and frostbitten heart
Oh love, what happened?
How did it all come to this?
It was not supposed to end up like this
I am alone in a tragic world of others
Living out days of never

These Eyes

Sever this kiss from me,
And take it with you
While you are at it,
Take these solemn eyes as well;
For they are only worthwhile having in your
Presence alone
Without you, there is no light
All that I am is perception
The perception of you
Without you, I am an empty observer
Uninterested in anything else

The Moment

Hand in hand the music stirs, quietly we move
I observe and I absorb all that is you
All that is both sacred and profane
I breathe in your essence, taking it in deep
Your scent infiltrates and infects my soul
You move me and strip me of my defense
I stand before you naked at the water's edge
Without hesitation, I slowly submerge
Your holy waters swallow me whole
The music stirs, quietly we move
Slowly at first, for fear that this is a lucid dream
on the verge of waking
The world grows dim and quiet as my focus
methodically narrows around you
It concentrates and gently frames you
Time stands poised and ready to jump back
to its full tempo
But it waits; as though to stare at the sight of me
staring at the sight of you
Both time and I are in awe of the moment
because we are one with the moment
The music stirs, quietly we move
Your fingers caress and breathe life into my
broken hands
My hands erupt with unexpected passion
Fear heralds the new dawn -- You, my love
I know now that nothing could ever be the same
For we have this moment now and forever
Nothing can take this from me
The moment is holy to me

The moment is enshrined in time itself
The moment simply... is
I know that to you this was just a dance
Maybe it was an excuse to be away from
another
Perhaps an act of mercy or worse yet,
an act of sympathy
But that matters little to me now
For in that moment, there was a little peace of
mind that I came to call my own
For in that moment, you gave me a chance to
forget all that I am
For in that moment
... I was with you

Icon in Flux

You are like a strange and beautiful religion
An icon in flux
You could raise the dead,
If only you felt the need to
I was fine until I felt your touch
I was unaware that I was asleep
until you woke me from my slumber
You beckoned fire into me and put motion
back in my flesh
Calling forth the Dragon did not help
The fire stirs deep within me now
Your face and your eyes

Omnipresent in my thoughts and in my clouds
You are the fever and the chill in my bones
It is like a ravenous curse
Non-stop and ever pursuing
I'm thinking of you
All I do these long bitter days is think of you

The Hue and The Ghost

I am not the product of fanfare
Nor am I the result of love
I am a coincidence
Fragile and singular
I stand alone
Even when I feel the touch of another,
I am alone
My barriers are great and vast
My shelter becomes my shell
In turn, my shell becomes my prison
I am alone
It takes a lot to get to me
Even more to get through to me
There is an ether of solitude
It binds and separates me from Heaven, and
Earth, and all theaters in between
I have seen and felt with great impunity
Still I have little in the way of recall
And it takes so much out of me to know,
That ... All that is; is exactly just that

Gustavo Lapis Ahumada

Nothing more and nothing less
Nothing sacred
I wait and wait for salvation
But I fear that it will probably pass me by or
just forget my face
I wait for grace to return
so that I may be seen again
Seen not for my fading presence,
but for inner strength and courage
Let grace open your eyes so that you may see
the real me; and feel my roar like that of a fiery
young lion adorned in golden robes
Let majestic strength, which I know and
recognize deep within me, make itself open to
your eyes and your heart only
Like you; my love, I am more than this mere frail
shadow of flesh
I am the hue and the ghost,
not just the emotive shell
I know that somewhere inside I am beautiful
even though my shell gives little or no hint of it
It does take faith
It takes the newfound faith of the faithless
As they come face to face with oblivion to see
the hue
To touch the ghost
I offer you no hope -- for I have no hope to offer
I only offer you strong arms to hold you down
when your storm hits
I offer you eyes, deep and dark, to guide you
through the tempest in your heart
Let us hold hands -- For the night is long

If I had your Kiss

Slowly I close my eyes
Tears cease to exist
I understand
Life is not perfect by design
You don't need all that I offer
Nor the little I can give
Tonight I believe in God
Tonight, I understand
This is just one of those things
I will not beg, nor will I harass
I am no stranger to disappointment
I have seen the fires of hell before
They do not scare me
I will do my best not to stare
Because I understand
I accept your decision cold
-- Bitter taste on my lips
I will not add to the turmoil
To your distress
I will bow out gracefully
I will give you peace of mind
I will respect all of your decisions
I understand -- nothing
This numbing feeling grows deep in my heart
As my hopes are slowly kissed and laid to rest;
Like a mother to a child
I will remember the dance
I will not forget the dreams
And I will always wonder
What nights would be like, if I had your kiss

Gustavo Lapis Ahumada

Walls

Tonight I stare gently at the waves
They ebb back and forth echoing the sighs in
my aching heart
I have come to terms with defeat
-- You don't want me
I can't say I blame you,
For what in God's name could I do for you
anyway?
I hear the Siren's song
It's calling, beckoning for me to enter her waves
Calling me to enter the long slumber cold
But I have been through this before
and there is no promise in that
Droplets of water caress my face
and for a moment, I picture your hands
Touching my face, healing my heart
My God, will I leave this place
devoid of true love?
Never knowing what it would be like
to kiss you?
To hold you in the rain?
To feel your hands on my face?
There is a great sadness here
I believe I have put the world to shame tonight
I don't see the justice of it all
Perhaps I deserve this somehow,
although I doubt it
For all my deeds, good and evil, have been
justified
The waves ebb back and forth

They reflect life, death and life once again
Tonight I call forth the Siren and I dare her to join me
Tonight I beckon her to my deep waters
So that I may be touched once again
My standards are high
Sometimes too high for most
I have spent too many years building walls
and destroying hopes

Downward spirals

Once again I am at the water's edge
This time I accept it all
I sense the boundaries ever strong
The barrier came down hard between us tonight
If my heart had a skull,
it would be crushed by now
If my soul had skin,
it would glimmer with indigo bruises
I surrender myself again to the waters of your sea
But there is no hope
I am the hue in motion
Gliding ever downward,
Nothing can save me now
Your eyes now see through me,
As though I no longer exist
Therefore, I do not
Your smile hits hard

Gustavo Lapis Ahumada

It is an anchor you willingly give to me
to help my descent
Life flows through me,
I am in constant motion
Downward spirals, but in motion nonetheless
Fires rage deep inside,
My laughter, mad and intoxicated
I raise my arms daring for more and more and more
The fires rage deep below the sea
I am on the verge of numbness
Nothing can save me now, Nothing
The fires still rage and all I can manage to do
is laugh - I have finally gone mad
This is life and there is no salvation
The madness consumes me -- The fire below your sea
The fires calm, but all is not perfect
Yet they settle into perfect harmony
Embers of madness are all that remain of me now
Do you remember me? The kiss?
The gentle smoke in our thoughts?
Will you remember or will you regret?
Now everything I am or was is like a strange shadow on
the moon
It's there - hidden and waiting
It is yours if only you put the effort to search for it
But I am afraid that it will barely be worth the trouble
when you find it
The fire goes to sleep deep below your sea
Shhh, quietly, no one to notice the last flicker
No one to sing a last lullaby
The beautiful becomes the beautiful
Shhh, it is okay you did nothing wrong

Deeper Kiss

Heaven's storm is over
The ground is moist, fresh from the rain
The scent of a clean spirit is in the air
The scent of purity -- of a better time
I hover above the puddles
Sometimes catching my reflection
Mostly trying to avoid it
All is calm now
Yet deep inside the hue, there is a waiting
I know it will go wrong again
There is a sadness and a truth
And the truth is the sadness
I am trying to put my thoughts to sleep
Peace of mind is too far away to grasp for
Something that will always be out of my reach
The thoughts of you have already entered
and trampled my aching soul
There is nothing you have not done to me
that hasn't been done to me before
By better, by worse
Or by you
There is a sense of release
At the hands of submission
I have no control over this
Therefore there is neither conflict
nor an attempt to fight it
My pride bleeds
I understand that I was not enough
But logic alone does little to calm the ghost
You and I came so close

Gustavo Lapis Ahumada

Sharing thoughts and touching lips
Now there is nothing
And it kills me with a slow, numbing death
Like the kiss of an asp near my soul
Your venom delivered with a kiss
Peace and tranquility fade
Like the thoughts of my touch to your skin
Like my lips on your back
Like my kiss deep in your mouth
Soon it will start again
The scent of your hair sends me into a mad
drunken stupor
I succumb to the lust at hand
I reach to kiss you -- a deeper kiss
But you are not there, my eyes open
The world is black

Creole Charm

Vile, wanting; you send for me
Wicked words and dirty hands
Lustful heat and dilated eyes
You summon me
Fiery black dream your hands demand
I refuse you with every part of me
But you hold the words,
The Creole charm over me
The wicked words your mother taught you
The same words she used on me
Glittering scars, sweet reminders of your
mother's lust
Streak my broken back like stars across black sky
Like always I cave,
My throat thirsts for you
I'm here now, do what you will
Make me hate you

Gustavo Lapis Ahumada

Palero's Night

Fresh rain on the ground stares at a lost soul
It reminds me of the dream I once had
On a slow barge, on a warm moonlit night
A powerful Palero's night,
mystical like purple dusk
Magic hangs heavy in the air
It is a night of in between worlds
The lone boatman, whom I can't see,
Navigates a rickety old barge with a single pole
Majestic slow strokes, like dreams upon smoke
All around me headstones, and crosses
Forgotten temples for the dead
A cemetery submerged under water -- waist deep
Wild vines everywhere and the vivid sense
of being watched
Heaven and the Ether, they watch
Drums, deep inside my chest, rumble silently
yielding no sound only emotion
Yellow eyes glowing,
rolling to the back of his head,
His gapping crooked smile lets me know
that he is in-between worlds
One foot here and one foot somewhere else
He says to me: "Beware of the Mad Unicorn,
for it is a tragic thing gone wrong"
The words move up and down my back like
Death's icy cold fingers
Fear races like wicked tongues of flames
skipping across my neck and down to my
hungry stomach

I can feel the creature staring at me
I think I see it -- I am afraid to look
It stares at a lost and scared soul
My eyes open, and the words echo
"Beware of the Mad Unicorn, for it is a tragic
thing gone wrong"
I look up and about me trying to get a bearing,
Trying to feel something
But I realize the dark truth,
for this storm is not over
This calm is just the eye of the storm
I look up through this portal to the heavens
and I see the stars
The moon and the angels all in awe or in shock
They stare down at me each helpless to do
anything, agony clear in their eyes
Something has gone wrong in creation
and we all know it
The calm is temporary
for the eye of the storm is on the move
I dread this place in the cold dark of the storm
I knew that your waters were deep and I knew
that your waters were cold
But I had no idea that it would be so dark down
here -- At the bottom of your sea
I turn a tear-glazed eye to the sky and I see the
bad storm rising
You are coming over soon, aren't you?
And soon it will be over
Inner peace is gone and the lights begin to fade
It is not bad enough that you have become
Consuming like ubiquitous dark sea

Gustavo Lapis Ahumada

No, now you must also become the harrowing
storm in my pale sky
The blackness comes
I have no strength to muster
I close my eyes and I hear the swelling of your
angry sea
Your scent heavy in the wind
It is all over
A Unicorn is laughing,
Somewhere in the dark of your bitter sea

So Much Better

I saw the kiss
It struck like a harpoon cruel and accurate
You kissed him
I felt the life gush out of me
Perhaps he was attractive, or better for you
Am I that unattractive to your eyes?
How could you not see me?
The real me?
I saw the kiss
Slowly he leaned toward you,
Eager with anticipation
His eyes met yours
His gaze dropped down to your lips
to make sure of his mark
Your stare focused in on his mouth
with an over-practiced reflex
White veils will never suit you
Your lips and his lips met
The kiss ripped, ecstasy for you both
The kiss tore right through me
If you wanted to hurt me -- That was overkill
There is an art to pain
A master's touch delivers the right amount
for the right result
But you went beyond the need
Pain and guilt are the weapons of choice
for the Beautiful
But the kiss, that was sheer cruelty
Was his kiss deep like mine?
Was his kiss as revealing as mine?

Does any of this make a difference?
I saw you kiss
He was younger I suppose and better looking
But did he notice your sea?
Did he call forth the fire?
Your fire?
I saw you kiss -- did you see me flinch?
Slowly, I slipped back out of the room –
Back into the fog and the illusion
Your betrayal tainted what was once holy to me
I took your kiss home that night
It stayed with me playing over and over in my
head
Your lips could do so much better

Monsters and Miracles

Breathe for me
For I have nothing left to exhale
Bleed for me
For I have no more blood to spill for you
Dance for me
For life itself has been drained from my shell
Sing for me
For my throat chokes on coins of copper
and shards of tear-stained glass
See for me
For my eyes expired the day I saw the truth
The truth between you and I
The truth that Monsters and Miracles
were only shadows
Shadows that I brought to fruition
Because I had nothing to hold on to
And all that I did have
Was simply was not mine to begin with

Gustavo Lapis Ahumada

Brilliance in Effect

Her smile, nothing short of radiant
Blinding strobes pale in comparison
Her smile is brilliance in effect
Like a modern messiah
She is ready to absolve
She is ready to offer an illusion
If only for the moment
She pours a drink
Her eyes, deep and focused,
always ready to forgive
Beautiful beyond words and beyond touch
She is exactly what some men dream of
and what some others dread
The music booms and the lights flash
But there is no show like the glow of her smile
Or softness of her eyes
But even I know that some people, like Angels,
are never meant to be touched
Some of us will always be out of reach
She and I are not too different
We are both predators of one sort or another
The only difference is that she is on one side of
the bar and I'm on the other
Beyond all else, she is wonderful
She is more than just a maternal figure
She is tenderness absolute in this cold world
She is a warm cove, a haven for lost souls
Brimming with deep sense of acceptance
There is nothing that could exempt the likes of
you or I from her heaven

There is almost nothing that she would not
forgive
She has a keen sense of understanding
For a moment, the world pauses
Smiles are exchanged and I can breathe again
I can't help to think that one day all of this
will be gone
No more club, no more music,
No more drinks from a master of her craft
One day my one and only confidant will no
longer be there for me
Love always crashes
The heavens turn
Friends eventually walk away
It is the way of things
It is what we are
What else can be more human?
But for the moment there is nothing better
Steady is her hand
She maneuvers her drink with cold calculation
Under a guise of warmth
She knows me, knows about me
Knows my pain
In her eyes I am the devil
Though fragile and still bleeding
I am the devil nonetheless
For every woe filled story that pours out of me
She's heard at least ten others caused by me
No judgments, not from her, not tonight
I stand before her stripped of everything
She lifts warm caring fingers to my face
as compassion embodies her

Gustavo Lapis Ahumada

Eyes upon my eyes, she smiles.
She smiles because she knows what I am
thinking
She knows my hateful thoughts and the black in
 my soul
"What am I doing here?" I torture myself over
and over again
She smiles again creating an illusion of tears
swelling in her eyes
She does her best to steer me away from those
dark unforgiving waters
She gives me a deep caring look saying:
"Don't do this to yourself ... not now."
In her eyes I am the devil,
A strange sad one at that

My Beautiful Full Moon

I don't think of you as often as I once did
You no longer caress my night sky
as you once did
When you were there omnipresent
and ever glowing
What was once constant is now occasional
There was seldom a night that expelled
your participation
You were always the Moon
Constant, with vigilance over my darkened skies
With a warm smile and warm eyes you nurtured
a decaying dominion
Now all that is left are bittersweet memories of a
Queen long gone
I don't think of you as often as I once did
You no longer caress my night sky
as you once did
When you were there omnipresent
and slowly fading
What was once Providence is now silenced
Once, you were always the Moon
Now you are like the Full Moon
Mysterious and Scarring
Infrequent and Occasional
Rarely provoking thoughts
But on occasions when you do,
It's all about you, my beautiful Full Moon

Patience and Process

It seems that every kiss taken
Leads back to the same place
Whether my fault or not
My fault mostly
Through a raspy maze of empty promises
In the end, I always end up here
In my cold corner
This time, it's different
This time I find no motivation
I have no reason to look again
I am not venturing forth anymore
I fail to see the carrot
I have lost my patience with the process

Autumn Sun, Winter sky

Through grated fence you trance down upon me
Pity in your eyes
Heavy like the anchors keeping you in place
Barren cold concrete reaches up through my feet
Gripping me by the throat, chocking life and hope
alike out of me
Autumn sun your halos play like awkward
magnificent winter's shackle
What happened? Did winter spirit snare you before
your due time?

Are you trapped, fading in this city's icy grip?
I think I am
Be strong autumn sun in your winter sky
We may be down, but we are not out
Even bitter wind, which mockingly slaps me
across my once tender cheeks, knows change is
about
Bear your sorrow and buy your time
Glory will soon be yours again

Love has Fallen

It is with heavy heart that my eyes open
My trembling hands do all they can
to muster strength
Strength now long gone
Like arrogance faded and torn
I see it in you
In your eyes
In your fading hands
Love has fallen
One must have Faith
How can I have faith?!
On bleeding knees, with wailing heart
I cry out
How can this be?
Love has fallen?
Tear this flesh from me let my soul pour
down to sulfur street

Gustavo Lapis Ahumada

Cold calculated life
Leave me tender and raw
I have nothing left to suffer for
With hair carelessly flung over shoulder
you walk away
Beauty you hoard around you
like Christmas ornaments black
Nothing sacred
If you - then all!
If you have done this,
You, perfect and warm
Then all are destined to
You are proof undeniable
Broken hearts ablaze
Tears like typhoon red bent on death
Your eyes, doll-like sobriety
Nothing moves you
I would swallow broken glass
To move you
To quench this fire
but nothing I do moves you
Steel, cold and slow, into me
Nothing can save me
It is with heavy heart my eyes dim
Love has fallen

My Familiar Place

My eyes have seen the pain
In the faces of people staring at me
My god, what do they see?
Is it worse than I fear?
My hands still remember
What it was like to fall
and the sweet taste of honey
That once dripped from tongue to tongue
Now I lay here once again
In my cold familiar place
My Heart, My chest
I can feel claw marks
Digging and burning into me
Like something trying to claw its way out
Clawing its way out of me
Desperate to leave this wretched place
This fallen house I call heart
My hands, they shake
My hands, once strong and magnificent,
cry a feeble "… Mercy"
And I have no pride
… I have no pride

Gustavo Lapis Ahumada

The Chrome Prophecy

The Chrome snuck into our lives
like a thief in the night…
Under the guise of comfort and entertainment
It killed us all one by one
The machine logic killed love
The machines killed that which was most
Human about us
The process of love
The Internet killed love
As long as the Internet exist
There can be no love
No true love
No love that will know peace
No love that will know comfort and security
Hear me young lovers, smash your machines
and embrace love!
For the machines will make you cold,
Like machines
The Internet has increased the human contact
ratio a million fold
Thus diluting the essence of love
Diluting the process of love
Diluting Humanity
Making us more and more like them
Soon you will Love by ratio
Then you will seek perfection
defined by a machine ratio
And you will turn to the machines to achieve
your cold ratio, your new standard
The machines will dictate beauty

Rational beauty
You will intake and partake in the mechanics of
Digital sin
The sin of mechanisms
You will violate your flesh for the sake of
Chrome
You will glisten with the fingerprints
of a new God
A digital God
This is not rhetoric
This is prophecy
Smash your machines
Smash everything
In the name of Love, smash everything
The Chrome Plague starts like this…

Death like Love

So here we are
Now I realize the sad truth
The smile that I have come to adore leads to
nowhere
The luscious lips that burned a path through a
once cold heart
Have been misjudged and overestimated
What I thought was hopeful
Was once again a mistake
A sad and embarrassing mistake
Honor among thieves
So I will say nothing
We stood shoulder to shoulder on so many
battlegrounds
So many broken hearts amongst us
We loved and killed with the best
Angels fell around us like rain in a deep forest
A forest that was sole witness to our song
The forest that saw our flesh intertwine
Flesh that knew death like love
But when I thought the time had come
It came only for me
Thank you for the perfect smile

The Ache of Your Bed

Suddenly, nothing matters
The pain and the stress have dissolved
Along with my strength and all flicker of hope
My will, like my breath, winds down
I exhale all strength
Like a million red butterflies
seeping out my skin
Your words, your lies - Nothing ever changes
You lay with me but your heart is always
somewhere else
The simmering ache in your haunted bed
has finally broken my back
Severing me from my heart
Severing me from my pride
You have not changed
You will never change

Sunshine

Lonesome eyes beneath sand reach for the sky
A sky now long gone and faded
Yellow sun burns a harsh orange
Marking time's sad passage
Wasted soul's mourning loss black and cold
Sun, regal orange and majestic,

Like love overwhelming;
shines no longer for me
You promised never to leave me
I waited so many years
Waiting to once again hear your voice
Your word, calcified and brittle
You never came back
You just went on
You never came back

Elements

The weight of the void lays heavy on my heart
Pressing, squeezing, extinguishing all that I am
I lay still at the bottom of your sea
There is a calm down here, a silence
I take measured deep breaths
Savoring the slow methodical burn
Your sea is cold and winter black
I can't tell whether my eyes are open or closed
Tears float upwards to a better place
Your sand, pale like the forgotten snow,
seeps through my aged fingers
Sand angels are all I can make here at the
bottom of your barren sea
The Dark and the Cold
The Loneliness
Elements of my reflection
Echoes of an inevitable destiny

Darkest Hour

If you can't come to me in your darkest hour
Then please don't bother when all is well
If you won't mourn with me by your side
I want nothing of your joyful celebrations
If you won't let my skin bear witness to your
beautiful tears
Then spare me the warmth of your smile
On hallow ground you and I once stood
and made promises
Promises that you now treat with convenience
I'm not here just for song and dance
I'm here to collect your tears as well
I mourn your disinterest, for it kills me
Move with me, Move for me
Set things right
Lets us put Heaven and the Stars back in order

This Life

Leading this life is hard
Watching those around me burn is hard
Once upon a time I kept my hands
and my heart to myself
Once upon a time I was cold and introverted
Out of touch and safe
I've should have stayed there

Gustavo Lapis Ahumada

Away from things
Away from your good heart
The rattling haunts me
The broken hearts that follow me
They remind me of my wicked ways
Like silver charms on a filthy rusted chain
I've should have stayed in the black of the sea
Away from good things
Away from you

Teeth

You, who steals my teeth in my dreamy slumber
Invisible deviant hand that reaches in me,
While dreams distract and promise false
Out of the blue, when least I expect it,
You do your deed
You steal my teeth
Serving as first and last warning
of black things to come
Without a shred of dignity –
You send me crawling back
Bleeding and humiliated
How could you do this to me?
You and your world
I'm putting an end to the madness
Somewhere in my heart
there must be a trace of strength
Something to rally the noble angels to my cause

One last time, one last hope
To save this battle weary and weakened
heart
But as usual, my cries fall on deaf ears
There is no hope
Inevitable is the beautiful
How could you do this to me?
With humble flesh, I forgave and I loved
Why couldn't you?

Doom

Sword sheathed and barefoot I enter your valley
Knowing that I will not escape
Knowing that there will be no victory
I do not waiver
Even though you are my doom
I do not waiver
Burning sand greets wounded feet with a hiss
Silver vipers and black destiny shadow my steps
mocking me
Cracked crucibles pour out foul promises
Knowing that I will listen
Knowing that I will swallow
I do not waiver
Even though this is the end,
I do not waiver
Pride sheathed and barefoot in your valley
Knowing no escape

For escape is an empty promise of things pale
and common
Knowing no victory
In the face of love,
there could never be victory
Why enter?
Why stay?
If you need to ask,
you have not understood
This was never about an outcome
This was never about victory
This was about love
In the face of love,
I did not waiver
Even though you were my doom,
I did not waiver...

Dust

Drained by the pull of your broken promises
So tired of the lies bleak and wounding
Take what you will from me
I had asked for nothing in return
Nothing but love
But all you did was bleed me
You took and you took
And when I needed you the most,
You were not there
You were too busy collecting charms
You adorned your hair with my tears
And wore my teeth on your chain
You broke that which could not be broken
And you did so with ill celebration
The black party of your soul
Leaving me to wilt and succumb to dust
But even humble dust will have glorious day
For dust returns home to the warmth
and comfort of Mother's womb
Even dust will eventually find its way back to
glorious stars
to its rightful place in the misguided heavens
And that which was broken will be whole again
Eyes that once adored you,
Now see you for what you really are
Lips that came to know your lips,
Are now moving on
The tongue that you knew so well,
Now splits and forks ready to deliver venom
Venom like disgust that you deserve so well

I wash my hands of this
Dust upon your eyes
Let your name be blood stained

Hymn

Somehow I knew
From the onset of it all
That you, you would be my Downfall
Why did I let myself go?
I will never know why,
But the dream, it was good and warm
Like a perfect sunset
I had finally come up from my cold dark place
For a chance at fresh air and love true
Only to find myself choking
Choking on splinters of despair and ash
So back with me,
Back to my forlorn sea
Where only fools lay to bleed
What you did,
What we had
Only a fool would take a maelstrom for granted
Thank you for the Siren song for which now
I call my own
The hymn that celebrates and plots
my internal collapse

The Ocean in my Bedroom

Thunder rolling backwards
Slowly creeping towards me
With great wet reverb or haunting delay
I can't tell where the rumbling blur begins
or where it ends
The immensity draws the breath from me,
Rattling my ribcage empty
Siphoning soothing hope and air alike
Brittle pale bones chaffed and grated,
Splinter beneath the weight of the hollow roar
The rumble smothers me
like angry lover's hands
The mysterious growl sends sharp icy ripples of
fear racing across my aching skin
It drowns my thoughts
Hands to my ears
Trying to stop what can't be stopped
There is no going back
My hands tremble, frail with fear
I have never known fear until now
Naked beneath an angry sky
Alone in a cold place
When will enough be enough?
I don't want you back
I just want to rest my head on your shoulder
I don't want to share my life with you anymore
I just want you to hold my hand for a little bit
I don't want to hear your voice again
I just want you to hush the thunder
The stillness in my house is louder than any

Thunder that any storm can throw at me
The silence is the ocean enraged in my bedroom
Somewhere in there I lay cold
I don't want you back
I just want you to brush the salt from my eyes
When will enough be enough my love?
The emptiness in my heart is my barren desert
The weeping in my soul tumbles forward,
like rolling thunder
The thunder of a door closing that echoes
forever for me
Night after night

Silence and the Ghost

This is who I am
This is who you are
This is who we are
This is why I burn
This is why there is no peace
Lay me to sleep beneath the Shimmering
and I will believe everything you throw at me
No strength for questions
I will swallow the ghost
I will be silent

Beneath a Void

So here we are
Twisted but not more than usual
Insane but functional
I have lost my compass
And you? You are just lost
If I bleed, would you stop to take a picture?
If I cave, would you laugh?
Your smile, showed a warmth I never knew
existed
Beneath a void dressed in blue,
I spiral out of control
Come with me, come with me
The possibilities are not endless
but they are promising
Who could understand you more than I?
In your voice I hear the code
It infiltrates all the dark that I am
Unlocking sad and wicked things within me
If I cave would you laugh?
Yes, you would
If I stand my ground would you regret?
I know I would and now I'm lost

Dead to Me

Bleeding hands on my burning temple
The one I built for you
Purple dust in the city of the dead
The one I razed for you
And now there is nothing
Now you are nothing
Now there is nothing left to bleed for
You are dead to me
Let fire rain down from the sky
I close my eyes
I wash my hands of this
Broken lips to my aching dream
The one I dreamt with you
Wasted tears in my gray house
The house I shared with you
And now there is nothing
Now you are nothing
Now there is nothing left to live for
You are dead to me
Let fire rain down from the sky
I close my eyes
I wash my heart of this
So human is your heart
Weakened by the stars in your eyes
And the false promise of security
Of a life in agonizing mediocrity
A Faith you betrayed
How I long to forgive and forget
You belong in a place like this
With someone like me

Just because you did nothing wrong
Does not mean you didn't do me wrong
You are dead to me
Let fire rain down from the sky
All along I should have known that
I have been long dead to you

To Sting Best and Deepest

What is Love, if not for the promise of
 Heartbreak?
Love stings best and deepest when all is perfect
At the point of least concern,
of least worry
That's when the other shoe always seems to
Drop like hammer on marble floor
Shattering the peace and rare calm in my soul
Silence is never just silence anymore
If anything,
it is merely the quiet eye of the storm
The in-between illusion that all is well
In between the fringes of the promise of love
and the bounds of certain loss

Gustavo Lapis Ahumada

Unhinged

Was it a word too much?
Was it one lash too many?
Or was it just time?
What unhinged my cage?
Foul spirit, you gnaw at my sanity
You have cost me a love beyond measure
Now my door swings open, unhinged
You forget who I am
Not who I was,
who I am
And the Serpent stirred,
eyes transfixed upon you
Seeing you for what you are
With guiltless pleasure,
I rain upon you
Paying you back tear for tear
for all that you've done to me
The backlash of your own venom
shatters your calm
sparking flame to your pale, deviant designs
With a good Merlot in hand,
I gladly watch you burn

My Cold Chair

Of all the souls in this miserable place
Yours was the last one I wanted to stain
Doubt everything about me
Doubt it as much as I do
But never doubt the sincerity of the moments
The moments when we succeeded in shutting
out the world and history
The moments when only you and I stood alone
floating above this sea of Mishap
If my filthy hands could raise the dead
I would
But to spoil is all my hands now know
As I sit back in my cold chair
I see the world through your eyes
and shame swells in me to a choking point
One, which I wish would not cease
But mercilessly releases me long enough
to catch my breath
For another chance to drown in my filth again
Let this chair creak amongst the smoke and
smoldering debris
Let this chair succumb, along with me,
to the ashes of my burning house
Let no fond word attach itself to my name
And this lonesome fire will quietly burn
Beneath a blackened sea
An ocean inked and marred, by all
that I have become
If not for my anchor in this place,
I would long be gone

Gustavo Lapis Ahumada

Sober

No matter what I say
No matter what I do
No matter how many dreams go unfulfilled
No matter how many tears burn down my face
No matter how many times
I cut your name into my flesh
No matter how hard
I try to reason with angels
No matter how many offerings I make
No matter how many heart-wrenching sighs
I release in your name
No matter how many times
I dream of you walking away
No matter how many times
I cry your name to the wind
No matter how hard my body aches for you
No matter how badly my lips burn for you
No matter how many times
I visit you in your sleep
No matter how many poems I write
No matter how many songs I bleed for you
No matter how hard I cry
No matter how much I have changed
No matter how much have I suffered
No matter how long I will suffer without you
No matter how many prayers I kneel
No matter how hard I try,
I still keep breathing
No matter what, you are never coming back

Prince of Fools

God, you and I have not spoken in years
Tonight we speak on strange terms
Love all you want,
but please stay out of my way
My heart shatters under the cold press of a lie
A lie like no other
I now live on my knees begging for an end
My eyes, yellowed with disappointment
I reach into my chest and yank out something
charred and dead
The fiery remains of what was once a good
and noble heart
I stare down at my burning flesh
ashamed and betrayed
I lift my burning heart to you as an offering,
to stop my pain
But you refuse to take it,
and there is no stopping the anguish
The memory of her smile grates broken glass
across my hands and feet
Her eyes once full of promise,
Now promise someone else
I bleed her name across my chest
So that I don't forget
I have lost love and only true friend
I take my burning heart and place it on my head,
A fiery crown
A crown of pain forged in pretense
I hate myself for allowing this to happen
I wear the fiery heart, my crown,

Gustavo Lapis Ahumada

Prince of Fools
If you won't silence me,
then please step aside
And let me silence love

Break my Heart

There is no love out there
Not with you people
Only one love I know
She tortures me constantly
Like I do the thousand
The thousand broken hearts left behind me
Behind me in a wake of destruction
Only one love I know
Only one love that has never abandoned me
Like the thousand
The thousand I have never abandoned
It's not my woman
Her heart is always somewhere else
It is not God, at least not tonight
Love?
There is no love out there
Except for my words
My song
My gift
My voice
Music, she is the only constant
Whether good or bad

There is no love out there
Except for this thing between heaven and me
And you people?
Well, you all break my heart
So excuse while I grab my guitar
God and I have some talking to do

Hope

Now that I lay here in this solemn place
I think of you and all my broken promises
I'm so tired of having to say sorry
This is my last goodbye to you
Give my kisses away to my family
Let them know that I thought of them
On this last cold moment
Tell them I died a happy death
Though you and I will know better
Know that I lay here with you,
always with you
Though there is no love in this world
There is love in my heart
Take my heart from me
Plant it somewhere warm
Let love come again

Gustavo Lapis Ahumada

This Crooked Hill

I wish you could take back what you said
But words do not rewind
I wish you could take back what you did
But kisses stain time and hearts alike
I'm so tired of racing up this crooked hill with
you and always falling
I'm so sick of letting you down
and cutting myself
I'm getting tired of always tumbling towards
certain heartache
At the end of the day, who's going to know?
All the things that you dreamt of
Dreams we held true and were worth
fighting for
A slow steady tempo is all that is left
To remind us of our loss
Of what we once were

A Breath Away

I no longer speak of love
The thought of the flawed concept burns
It burns and sanitizes all that I am
Why give me a heart if I cannot be with you?
A love with you
A love clean
Free of Sin
Free of Distortion
Free of Judgment,
Free
A love like that is always out of reach
Like lost horizon on ocean's edge
A love like that is always for someone else
A love where I can rest my head
Close my eyes
Know that all is well
A love like that is always out of reach
for someone like me
A love like that is always a breath away

Gustavo Lapis Ahumada

At the Foot of my Bed

Softly, gently, you crept into my bedroom
Gliding on rose petals guided by tears
You sat at the foot of my bed
Once again, at the foot of my bed
My eyes sensed you before I sensed you
So I awoke to find you there,
at the foot of my bed
I sat up, tears swelling waiting for a cue
You no longer hover over me,
Not even in my dreams anymore
You just sit there
and stare at me
The sigh in your heart is hidden from me now
Yet it deafens me to no end
Your eyes tell of oh so many things,
You are the Siren that answered the call
But you have nothing to say to me
This silence kills me slowly
I can't change anything
Not who I am, and definitely not you
If I could I would surrender all that I have
But all I have are sighs,
at the foot of my bed

When the Stars Give Way

Will love ever be just?
Will it ever play fair and be noble like
the balance between Earth and Sea?
Will it ever give up its predatory nature?
When will love be like a soothing
Like a body of warm water?
Love will be love
Until the stars give way

Hands

I'm not sure I know how to do this
I have never asked for this before
What's the word? Help?
Help, is it?
Always have been cursed with Pride
Help me - Be with me, hold my hand
Don't have to stay with me
Just be with me while I gather my strength
I am lost
Lie to me if you have to
Let false hope to prop up what's left me

Stand

I embrace the storm to come
My chest is empty and hollow
like a poor man's kettle
I have no tears left in me
because I am done with it
Done with this thing I have clung to all my life
Love is the constant division
Between Heaven and Earth
Tonight my veils giveaway
Eyes closed
Heart and soul bound by faith
With arms wide open I welcome your sting
I welcome the cold of your steel
I know no fear anymore
All that could be taken
Has been taken
Let me love eternal
Let me love true
No matter what the price
For I rather perish knowing that I took a stand
Then to live a life sheltered and little

Mirror and the Radio

Another night slips by me,
lost in this mess I call my life
Like innocence in time's lonesome march
Drinking in someone else's bed does little to
silence the echoing hurt of you
A song comes on the radio
raining razor reminders of you down upon me
The night grows cold and dim
leaving me stripped of flesh and warmth
Solemn tears glide quietly down my face
The night grows colder still,
like winter nights on bleakest days
The thought of you breathing with someone else
kills me with every second that passes
The song plays on forever
indifferent to my wound
My body shakes at the thought of you
with someone else
The breath sneaks from me,
dreading another breakdown
Not another one, not again,
Not without you
This sorrow runs forever,
like the stars in a runaway sky
Mourning is all I know of Love
The thought of you has become a fever
burning steady night after night
Offered prayers I bled out in vain
Always fall upon cold and indifferent ears
Wishes fall pale like the pieces of me that now

litter the marble floors of a long lost
Forgotten Temple
A broken heart knows no pride
But what can be more noble than a broken heart?
Death ignores me,
no matter how I hard I weep
And the song keeps on playing on the radio
Mocking my heart
Laughing at my soul at every turn
It's the anthem of the fall of a once good man
No more celebrations,
No more coronations
Only a soft song to forget me by
Bitter dust and ash
Is all that is left of a life,
The echoes of a love
That was once so clean and true

King

I am King
And you, you are my crown
I am the Papa King
King of the dinosaurs
King of the Elephants
King of the Pumpkin patch
And you, you are my Pumpkin
You are my crown
When I get too serious,
you lean forward
tilting off the side of my head,
Reminding me of who I am
Silly like you
A kid just like you
You are my crown
You are my joy
Stay little
Stay with me
I hope not to let you down
But sometimes even kings are not perfect
One day you will be Queen
Queen of the dinosaurs
Queen of the Elephants
Queen of your own Pumpkin patch
You will have your own Crown
and your own Pumpkins
I hope I get to see your crown,
and your pumpkins
You are the best part of me
You are the best part of Mother Mermaid

Don't forget me
Stay little
Stay with me
Even though new tides may guide you away
to a new land
To new home
Don't forget me
Stay little
Stay with me
I am king only because you are my crown

Every Dream Shattered

Cold rain bears down on me
with Heaven's full weight
Each raindrop hammers down on me a reminder
of every heart I have broken
and every dream that has shattered
The shimmer and gloss on the ground is a
lonesome reflection of disappointment
Drudging slowly forward to the drum-like
Murmuring echoes of hope collapsing
Cold wind and dead leaves are all that are left of
a life wasted in sin and vice
But then I think of you and realize that there has
to be something more to all of this
Something greater than myself or the sum of my
misadventures
How horrible could I have possibly been if you
are still with me?
You are the beautiful flaw in this masterpiece of
misery and ruin
You are the proverbial silver lining to my
cloudy day
If true love is a journey
then surely you must be the compass by which
such beauty guides itself

Gustavo Lapis Ahumada

Dare my Heart Ponder?

Dare my heart ponder?
Love?
It is so difficult to sound genuine
with this cold medium
Life, my cold medium
Know this, if anything ever, know this
I am moved by you
Like frothy sea by sudden gale
I am moved by the possibilities
you summon within me
Once again, the illusion of hope seduces me
The promise of promise smiles upon me
It offers a gentle hand
It is the gravity that gently calls
and calmly pulls me in
I believe in you
I believe in what we could be
I believe in fire
The fire I feel for you
The fire I feel when I am with you
Only with you
... One foot off the ledge
… Leap with me?

Show Me This

Show me fire like Supernovas running wild
Show me stars not afraid to crash and burn
Give me what I see in you
Give me what I can sense in us
Give me Love
Magnificent love

Fear

It is not gravity that binds me to the ground
It is the fear that I would fly after you
if I saw you in the clouds
It is not the sun in the sky that blinds me
It is the fear that your smile is for someone else
It is not the Sea above me that keeps me rooted
in this dark place
It is the fear of what I might see if I dare to
surface
It is not the Fire in my heart that enslaves me to
my solitude
It is my fear that my heart will burn alone
It is not the army of a thousand men that keeps
me from you
For no army of Heaven or Earth could keep me
from you

Gustavo Lapis Ahumada

That In-between Place

I woke up feeling lost
and somewhat still in a daze
My Soul still firmly rooted in that beautiful
Place we came to call our own
That in-between place
The memory of last night's passion
Plays relentless within me
The scent of your mouth still lingering on my
yearning fingers
You have changed me
Things have changed
The world is no longer the same
Put your hands on my face
Tell me that you are as real as the rain
And I will believe you

Noise

The actions of others make noise
Irritating and malevolent noise
The black noise
The noise of insanity
Echoes of the insane
Like jet engine turbines growling at my ears
Screaming, screeching; bleeding my ears
Tearing at my soul
Bleeding me
The emerging clamor engulfs me
in a whirlwind of stupidity
It smothers life from me
Black din to strangle me beneath its heaviness
The din turning my sanity into insanity
Vulgar rant, green and ill with vile intent,
Drowns the good in me
The noise suffocates me
I see no end
I see no end until I see you
You blanket me in pause
Your name is fortitude and serenity
Your name, is a good word
A word to calm the storm
To hush the din
Your name is a sweet melody,
Like a lullaby
Your name soothes me
You are here, now all goes quiet
With you by my side, I can dream again

Gustavo Lapis Ahumada

The Ghost on my Tongue

You are in my thoughts
Not on rare occasion like blue Moon
Or perfect warm afternoon
But rather constant like ocean vast
And clouds ever glowing
Noble and unreal to my standards
For I have never experienced a love
or a nobility like yours
Though harsh life has rendered you cold to the
naked eye
You are tender
Tender, like a ghost on my tongue
Though your heart still wrestles razor wire
of callous winters past, you are smooth
Smooth, like a shadow on my skin
Though victim to many cold nights
You are warm
Warm, like a glimmer of hope
Casting a gentle smile across my battered soul
Know that I love you
Though gray days may seem like I am not with
you, know that I am
Nights of broken glass and fiery upheaval
know that I am still yours
For even in chaos there is love
A Love that knows no compromise
For only you breathe fire in me
You are like a ghost on my tongue
Sweet shadow of promise
I'm afraid to swallow for fear of losing you

Things

I can't tell anymore
Things are happening around me
I don't know if these things are good things
or bad things
The slow waters wash away my possessions
The things I have known all my life
Are worlds collapsing in on me?
Around me?
Or is this world sliding off me,
Like a cocoon off a newly fashioned Moth
A newly formed me?
But nothing is real
Things are not real
Maybe I'm not real
But this thing I feel for you
Yeah, it's real

Scarlet Agenda

Scarlet chemicals in you arouse
Foolish hope in me
What strange motive moves you?
Is it Love? Could it be love? Love like me?
Your agenda, hidden and slick,
It scares and ignites strange fires in me
In you there are new definitions to be defined

Gustavo Lapis Ahumada

Sessions

Let us dance and drink away this night
of shimmering blue
Let us love ourselves to sleep
So that when we awake we will be
in each other's arms
Tranquil, sated and safe
And we will wonder in love,
lost in an ocean of golden nectar,
which part of the night was a dream,
and which session of the passion was best

Fireflies

Where have you gone?
To that place where the fireflies wont find you?
Let your dreams blue guide your way
Can you hear my gentle song in the wind?
Let it find you and guide you back to my arms
My ocean is empty without you

Coming Home

Calm the sea for it is true
I am coming home to you
That which I once feared
is now good
This is what I was meant to be
I am coming home to you
Turn away from the stars
For they no longer shine
I will let go of this sky
For it no longer means anything to me
Not without you
Back with me,
back into the sea
I am coming home to you my love
Once again at the bottom of the sea
This was no place for me
The water cold,
solely knows this wretched me
Takes her time engulfing me
Taking me home
Once again at the bottom of your sea
Eyes to heaven
Sweet water pours over what is left of me
I am coming home to you

Gustavo Lapis Ahumada

Because I am in Love

Let them come
One by one
Let them come
Let them sharpen their dirks and forked tongues
Let them ready themselves for my flesh
I fear nothing, not today
Let them vie for a good spot
For a good angle on me
I need no Armor, not for the likes of them
I will stand naked before the horde
I will fear nothing, because I am in Love
In love, my soul is the superior weapon.

Roar

My thoughts are with you and know
in your heart that I am with you true
Somewhere between the Fog and the Doubt
Beneath the veil of darkness,
like a glimmer of hope
Hope with a beautiful voice
Not a whisper, not a murmur, but a roar
A Roaring Thunder of promise
Like a million Silver-Hoofed Stallions
Galloping across the Gold laden streets
of an ancient city

Words

Trivial secondhand words will never do
Never for someone like you
Fiery lover of warm skin and somber eyes
Failed Paradigms and Archetypes do no justice
Only the sincere reserve of words will do
No soul has ever felt what I feel for you
No saint has ever known passion the likes
you ignite within me
No catastrophic lover has kissed as sweetly
as I have with you
I alone hold the key to an ocean
A reserve of words fathoms deep, as it is wide
I hold the key in my ardent words when I draw
near your soul
It is in my mouth when I glide over the subtle
straits of your neck
It is in my words when I speak of you
The key, I hold in my hand when I hold your
hand and caress your skin
Trivial secondhand words will never do
Never in a million years for someone like you
You summon words unknown to me
Speaking in tongues, the new language of love,
True Love
Words that can only exist in a place like Heaven
From Heaven, to my heart,
From my heart to my lips
From my lips to your ears
In heaven there is a blissful ocean of words
Just for you and I

Gustavo Lapis Ahumada

Cold of the Black

Life, this gray tasteless march
Slow and dastardly
Grinds on like bored lover's
idle conversation
You have left me cold and confused
Dazed by the worthless compensation of it all
Worlds I knew once warm have imploded
leaving me fragile and covered in tears
like shattered glass
I have lost my faith in People,
I have lost my faith in Love
Slowly I submit to the cold of the tide
There is no will to hold breath
No use in hesitating,
Prolonging the inevitable
The water is cold; I can feel the bones in my
feet splinter and shatter
I think of how I got here,
The misadventures of a sinful heart
Deep inside I know that I deserved it,
All of it
The water rises higher
splitting bones upward across my shell
I have no more time in me for dwelling –
It is gladly over for me
The water takes me in,
A strange act of mercy
I accept for there is no choice but to accept
Eyes forced open, I don't want to miss a thing
I don't want to miss a thing

Slowly comes the end,
My soul waits to exhale
And in the darkest moment,
Of the darkest hour
… A hand
Out of nowhere, a hand plunges
It plunges fighting current and sense,
Diving into the cold of the black
The hand snakes down into the cold of the water
The hand finds my hand,
cold, battered, void of will
The hand yanks what's left of me out of the
Cold hungry water
The hand throws me back into the mix,
Back to the shores of stability
A mouth upon my mouth forcing air, hope and
sensibility back into my shell
Hand and mouth now force me to draw in
another breath
New breath
My eyes open, and there I see you
I see you and your black hair
I see you and your pale skin
I see your legs, like a pinup dolls'
I see your burning lips that kiss so so well
And your blue blue eyes
Indigo blue eyes, which see the gaping wound
in my chest
A wound raw and deserved,
vivid with fresh tears
And stale deception
I struggle with words

Gustavo Lapis Ahumada

Only to hear you hush my reserve away
You tell me with calm, warming voice
"No need to draw lines, no need for
a new plan… Just sit back and breathe"
Not the end I expected
Probably not an end I deserved
You stand majestic over me like Heaven's gate
Holding me in your arms
Forgiving and loving
Cold and weary I listen to your voice,
and I try to forget how I got here in the first
place
In your eyes,
a warm promise of something good
A promise of something exquisite

The Last Torrent of our Sins

Last night parts of Heaven and Earth merged
The parts that are seldom spoken of
And somewhere in the middle,
you and I came to kiss
Me, still bleeding and reeling from my hard
lesson learned
You, with your healing hands
and your broken heart
Together, we found a little bit of solace in this
fiery place
We held hands, waiting for the storm to hit
The last torrent of our sins
We do not walk like angels, because we are not
But we never deserved what they did to us
They circled with a hateful swirl of
disappointment and pain
It is you and I and them,
All of them,
The black swirl
The ones who lied,
The ones who took us for fools
The ones who tore into us
The ones who failed us when we needed
them the most
The ones who never said goodbye
It is you and I and the fruit of our decisions past
We must own that, which we fear,
So as to no longer fear it
Where are we going?
I have no idea

Gustavo Lapis Ahumada

Promise?
I have no strength left for promises
Hope? I have lost, but I sense an uprising
I sense it every time I look into your eyes
The pain and the fog lift
The path becomes clear
In the face of the enemy I lay down my sword
For I accept that it was my own doing
For it is my final and ultimate act
It is my way of finding peace
There is strength in submission
You lay down your sword beside mine
For you see what I see
The need to go no further
The ultimate sacrifice,
The last kiss goodbye
It is just you and I as the black swirls in
Our tears mingle and settle in the deep
Deep at the bottom of the ocean cold
I don't know what will happen
All I know is that the journey
will be something beautiful

If the Sea were to Sway

Gently, I move along,
whirling, smiling
In my head, a subtle song
My feet barely touch the ground
I'm not part of this place anymore
How I remember those sad days entrenched
in constant heartbreak
Days desolate black and long before you
Now seem like a lifetime away
If the stars were to gleam one final time
I know you would want me by your side
If the Sea were to sway, I know you would want
 me there with you as well
It is as though everything has led me to you
And every price paid
was well worth the suffering

This Day

This day opens new and majestic like monarch
butterfly with wings of fire and pride
Deep breath in my lungs charges my soul with
fresh resolve and innocent strength
It is not the mere golden dawn that rejuvenates
my cold spirit
It is knowing that this day,
Is the day that you will be with me

Gustavo Lapis Ahumada

And cold nights that once muffled my soul and
laid into me like slithering landslide black
will no longer suffocate this fragile frame
This day
This day will be a day of Love
Glorious love

Promise

Your eyes are a solid promise of a life to come
Blue in depth and in glory
Heaven holds nothing over you
Your lips burn a steady fiery red flame
A crimson lick of a life defined by flesh
Kisses that echo of an underworld long dormant
A time when life was ruled by myth and love
This is the dream of lovers
This is the dream I have feared all my life
It is what I fear to wake from
But you are here now and all is well
Your skin now a blur of alabaster and serenity
Blinding me, blinding me with sheer promise
No longer knowing where I end
No longer knowing where you begin

Sea of Misplaced Souls

There is the word
The word is love
The word is hope
The word is both
The word is a path that leads to a sacred place
A place of sheltering fog and subtle light
Me? I was lost
Lost in a sea of misplaced souls
Held down my by a thousand anchors
Always holding on to fruitless intentions
Then out of nowhere - Your eyes
Your eyes show me who I truly am
There is nothing your eyes could not forgive
I'll do all I can to keep you from turning away
Nothing I wouldn't do to keep you smiling
With your kiss I can deflect a thousand arrows
I see you, only you and your mouth
With your mouth, I find my true voice
Your mouth delivers me
Your mouth is salvation
Your mouth drives me
Your mouth is the switch
I let go and something ravenous now takes over
Your lips beckon me
I thrust forward
Lips upon lips our tongues entwined
There is no escape
There is no tomorrow
There is just you and I
In this Sea of misplaced souls

Gustavo Lapis Ahumada

Beauty and Strength

I never thought I would see the day
The day when blue eyes would move me so
I stare at you and I am mesmerized
As though I have discovered something new
Something pure
Something luscious
To think that once I was scared
To think that once I was afraid
of what was to come
Now I let your eyes ignite the way
The way to a good place
I thought I knew beauty
Now I know beauty
I thought I knew strength
Now I know real strength
Your blue eyes reign over my dominion
Like the celestial grace of an age long past
Like the sky over a humbled and battered land
Like an ocean above my watery grave
Like truth in a whirlwind of lies
Like beauty in the fog of corrosion
Like you my love, like you

My Beloved

Fear not
Doubt not
Worry not
For you are Red Wine and Cheesecake
beneath an autumn night
Even if this tide should turn
I will be with you
Listen to the timbre of the silence between us
It is not a feigning wail dusted in sorrow
But rather a slow deep breath drawn
before our next leap
Fear not
Doubt not
Worry not
For you are Vegas and all her Glory
beneath an Ocean of Stars
I am with you,
No matter what
I am with you

Gustavo Lapis Ahumada

Indigo Girl

You, now so out of place
Lost, you, look to the winds
Find your bearings
Find you courage
Where have you gone?
This life now is cold and so uninvolved
Find your faith,
Find yourself
Come home,
Come find me
Sad little girl with Indigo eyes
Come home
Come home
If I could take it all back,
I would
This place holds little magic without you
Come take my hand
Inhale deep and invigorating
Count backwards lets reset this accident
I can feel the Autumn air dancing on our skin
I can almost taste your kiss
I can feel your smile upon me
Count backwards with me
Three
Two
One...

Faster Cat

The Sun sets on your Paris Street
You are the red talk of the town
How could you not be?
Mount your machine,
Your Italian machine
Set your fires and break your hearts
Dazzle them
All of them
As you quickly whiz by them
Blinding them
All of them, on your Italian machine
They will leer at you
Barely catching a trace of that infamous sharp
grimace
Those heartbreaking crimson lips
Or those infamous Black lined,
practically indigo eyes
And they
All of them
Will raise their fists in anger
Screaming at you
Trying to stop you
Trying to catch a glimpse of you
You, blur of love
Swirl of beauty
Your fingers stroke and control your machine
With tongue to cheek you burn rubber
Through the smoke and the dust
That you will, oh so elegantly,
kick up to their faces

Gustavo Lapis Ahumada

They
Them
All of them will wonder
"Just who the Hell does she think she is?!"
As you quickly whiz by them

The Good Rain

Eyes forward little girl
The good rain comes
I love you, I miss you
Even though sometimes I feel that you're not
with me
Even though I fear that your heart wanders
Even though I can see the echo of kisses meant
for someone else still in your eyes
Even though I can taste the bitterness
of your broken heart on your lips
I cannot undo what has been done to you
Either you are with me or you are not
Come what May, Come what May
I hold no fear in my heart
Because there is no room for it
I am fearless
I am invincible
Do your lips miss me? Me?
My lips miss you
... Only You

My Wicked Garden

Night, and the music was soothing
We came to know each other so much better
I took your hand and lead you to a special place
Into my wicked garden
You sighed, overwhelmed by the tragic beauty
The sadness and the passion of it all,
as I set you free in my wicked garden
Barefoot, you ran laughing and swirling,
lulled into a love-crazed stupor
Your pale skin summoned things in me
The Moon and your skin danced,
singing out loud
calling forth something dark and beautiful
It's a beautiful night
A beautiful night for changes
Your eyes turn to me
But you don't see me any longer
You see something else
Under the moonlight of confusion,
your smile diminishes
Confusion yields to concern
Concern gives way to fear
and a strange kind of lust
My pupils dilate, as I focus on you
My vision blurs and magnifies,
colors jump alive
I can feel your heart beating, deeper and faster
The glint of sweat on your neck
is enough to ignite me
I pounce!

Gustavo Lapis Ahumada

You scream as you run madly through my
wicked garden
Your fear taunts me
You, pale gliding over my lush greens
You run, but you want me to catch you
My mouth tingles in anticipation
Over your shoulder, you grace me with a glance
An acknowledgement,
You know you're mine
You smile and I pounce again
This time flesh upon flesh
Flesh of my flesh
Deep into your neck,
Your mouth,
My tongue coils around you
and every part of you
Eyes open and close
gaping mouth in sheer ecstasy
Teeth into your flesh,
your nails into mine
We find death over and over again
In pools of honey and nectar we lay
Until the sun comes up,
in my wicked garden

Love Beneath the Sun

Celestial events by your side
With your eyes to comfort me
An Ocean of pain beneath me
A sky full of hope somewhere above me
And you,
Always you by my side
Come storm ever howling for you do little
to me other than drive me to love's arms
No Sunset will ever be the same
Sharing kisses
Sharing wishes
In a body of water that understands
In a fluid body of calm
The water will balance the wrong
The forest will hide us from a world
No Sunset will ever be the same
I will never be the same

Take Me

So many beautiful dreams bled or suffered
in the name of love
No matter how grand or noble our intentions
were; we somehow always failed
You and I – Always here, crushed beneath
weights of despair
No more my love

Gustavo Lapis Ahumada

Don't look back
Don't waste anymore time on this cruel thing
That goes on and on
This is the place where we take it all back
Dance with me and lets move on
These words
This place it is just for us
Let's find our way back home my love
Back to that once forgotten place
Where golden columns meet sweet greens
Come take my hand
Come take me
Just like love
Crushing and clean
Let the cold shadows of yesterday disperse
For those days are now long gone
Wipe away your solemn tears
Eyes forward to a new day
Love is calling once again
Let this sorrow slip off
Like silk scarf across a velvet sky
A new day is calling
Lets not waste anymore time
Come with me to this new world
To this new place
A place where we will start all over again
Our love,
Oh so strong, like winter desert skies
Will bloom and thunder
With the fury and passion of a thousand storms

November Dawn

Wish I could breathe you in
Hold you in my chest
Close to my heart
Beneath a winter sky
Like Monarchs in November dawn
Color wings against cold gentle breeze
Gold upon gold, Rare
On the verge of demise
Beautiful butterfly at the wrong time
But no time can be wrong by your side
Tragic
Limited dream with unlimited thirst to quench
Your kiss will echo long after you are gone

Gustavo Lapis Ahumada

Glide over Stars

Walk with me
Like me
Barefoot through this valley of vipers
Let them hiss vile and covetous
Let them rattle impotent cries
You are with me
So I know no fear
Kisses like the living
Romance like the dead
Purple flowers instead of red
Vipers amongst vipers
We are who we are
Which is why they tread sour ground
And we glide over stars

A Prayer of Gratitude

Never forget that once upon a time
there was nothing but sorrow
Never forget that once,
cold nights seemed without end
Never forget the thousand souls
that stood in our way
Never forget the Void that once loomed heavy
over all horizons
Never forget that things were not always this
good
Never forget and rejoice
For it is with a clean heart that we remember
And it is with a clean heart that we are grateful

Lightning Source UK Ltd.
Milton Keynes UK
17 February 2011

167696UK00003B/2/P